CW01096038

A girl called Madonna

A girl called Madonna

A Popjustice Book
Illustrated by David Whittle

First published in Great Britain in 2006 by Friday Books
An imprint of The Friday Project Limited
83 Victoria Street, London SW1H 0HW

www.thefridayproject.co.uk
www.fridaybooks.co.uk

Text © Peter Robinson 2006
Illustrations © David Whittle 2006

ISBN – 10   0 9548318 7 X
ISBN – 13   978 0 9548318 7 5

British Library Cataloguing in Publication Data

A catalogue record for this book is available
from the British Library

Designed and produced by Staziker Jones
www.stazikerjones.co.uk

The Publisher's policy is to use paper
manufactured from sustainable sources

This book belongs to

_____

I am ____ years old

My favourite Madonna song is ——————

When I grow up, I want to be ——————

Here is my autograph!

_____

This is Madonna. She is very pretty.

You can call her Madge.

Madge has a lawyer and a manager, an agent and a chef, three nannies, an assistant, and a driver and a jet, a trainer and a butler and a bodyguard or five, a gardener and a stylist.

Do you think she's satisfied?

She certainly should be! Madge is the best and most famous singer in the whole wide world.

Madge has been singing for a very long time.

Experience has made her rich.

Madge also likes to act in films.

This has not made her quite so rich.

Once upon a time a very long time ago, Madge was not famous.

But even when she was a little girl growing up in America it was her dream to be a star.

Who could have thought that the dream might one day come true?

It all started when she discovered that she could dance!

Madge was so good at dancing that she went to a special school, just for people who could dance!

She was particularly good at ballet.

One day her teacher told her: 'Go to the big city. There you will become rich and famous.'

Madge liked this idea, so she packed her bags!

Madge liked the city.

She liked the sweet sensation of dancing in the discos, but she still wanted to be famous.

One day she met a man.

The man said that he would take photographs of her, and that it would make her a star.

Unfortunately, Madge's clothes fell off!

One day Madge sang a song.

It was a happy song about going on holiday.

Luckily many people liked it and Madge was finally a star.

A lucky star!

Every time Madge sang a song, she looked a bit different.

Sometimes she would get a new dress or a new haircut.

But you could always tell it was Madge because Madge was the only singer in the world who was so interesting and so clever.

One time, Madge sang a song about feeling like she had never been kissed.

Lots of people thought this was odd because Madge had kissed lots of people.

Even Madge thought this was quite funny!

A few years later, Madge made a big book. It was full of lots of pictures of kissing.

In one of the pictures Madge even kissed someone's FOOT! How smelly!

But because Madge was so clever, she could talk about kissing without giggling or being silly.

Madge was so important that other people stopped being silly too. Madge changed how people thought about kissing.

For a while it seemed as if people forgot that Madge was a good singer.

Fortunately, it was not long before Madge remembered how important music was.

It made people come together.

Just like kissing!

One day Madge met a man called Guy. Guy was English and made films for a job.

She got to know him in a special way. He made her feel like a queen on a throne.

They got married!

Madge decided that she was bored of being American and wanted to be an English lady.

She started to drink a special magic potion to make her more English.

It worked!

On her 45th birthday, Madge went horseriding.

Whoops! Madge fell from the horse.

She hit the ground with a big bang.

Lucky Madge got better very quickly.

In fact it was no time at all before Madge was back where she felt most at home – dancing!

So that is how a girl called Madge became famous and brilliant.

She is still very pretty and a very good dancer.